Awarded for excellence
to Arts & Libraries

Kent
County
Council

The Natural History Museum

Animal Close-Ups

Fish

and other sea creatures

Barbara Taylor

OXFORD

UNIVERSITY PRESS

OXFORD
UNIVERSITY PRESS

Great Clarendon Street, Oxford OX2 6DP

Oxford University Press is a department of the University of Oxford.
It furthers the University's objective of excellence in research, scholarship,
and education by publishing worldwide in

Oxford New York

Athens Auckland Bangkok Bogotá Buenos Aires
Cape Town Chennai Dar es Salaam Delhi Florence Hong Kong Istanbul
Karachi Kolkata Kuala Lumpur Madrid Melbourne Mexico City Mumbai
Nairobi Paris São Paulo Shanghai Singapore Taipei Tokyo Toronto Warsaw

with associated companies in Berlin Ibadan

Oxford is a registered trade mark of Oxford University Press
in the UK and in certain other countries

British Library Cataloguing in Publication Data available

Paperback ISBN 0 19 910786 6

1 3 5 7 9 10 8 6 4 2

Printed in Hong Kong

Contents

About this book
This book takes a close look at fish and other
animals that live in the sea or on the shore.
It shows how their body shapes help them to feed,
move and survive in a world of water.

I am a silvery sea bass.

I am long and thin with a
pointed nose. My shape helps
me swim fast. I use my tail to
push myself through the water.
I hunt other fish.

When I was young,
I swam with other
young sea bass.
This protected me
from enemies.

My skin is covered with overlapping, bendy scales.

I breathe using the gills on the side of my head. They are covered by a scaly flap. Water flows in through my mouth and then out over my gills.

I am a bright yellow tang.

I live on coral reefs in warm oceans. I have two sharp spines near my tail. I lash my tail from side to side to cut my enemies' flesh.

My razor-sharp spines are hidden in a groove by my tail.

I use my small biting teeth to scrape plants off coral and rocks.

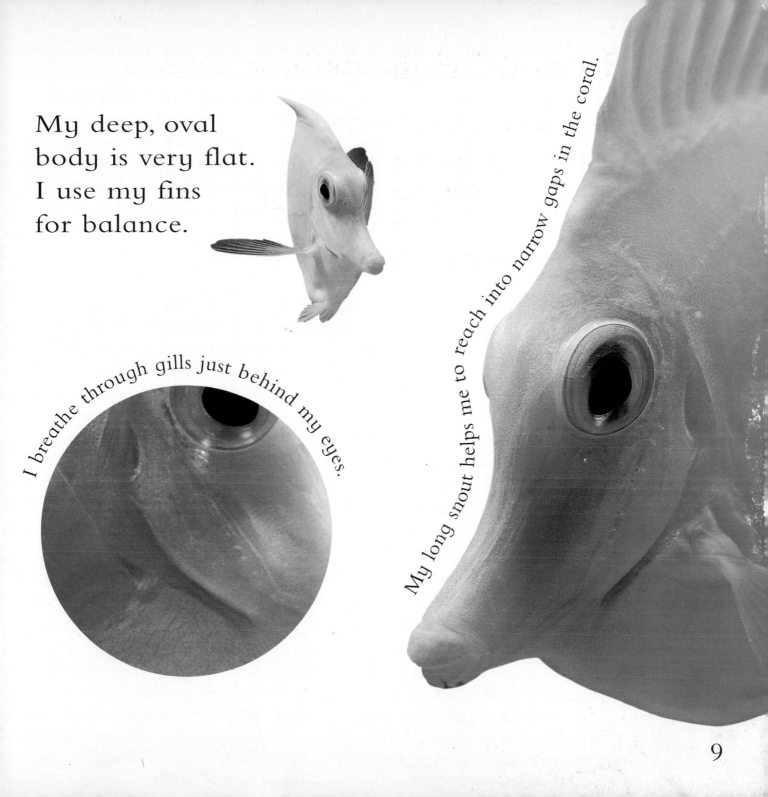

My deep, oval body is very flat. I use my fins for balance.

I breathe through gills just behind my eyes.

My long snout helps me to reach into narrow gaps in the coral.

9

I am a speckled flatfish.

I am called a top knot. My fins are round the edge of my flat body. My underside is pale, with rows of muscles. They help me to swim.

My top side is brown, with spots and blotches that help me blend in with sand and gravel on the sea bed.

My eyes are both on the same side of my head – the top.

I am a spotty pufferfish.

I live in warm seas. I do not have scales, but my skin is bumpy.

My spotty skin warns that I am poisonous.

My teeth are stuck together so they look like a bird's beak.

I use my fins to steer with, to balance and to slow down.

I can puff up my body with water or air, so my enemies cannot swallow me.

11

I am a leafy sea dragon.

I am a kind of pipefish, but the strange flaps all over my body make me look like seaweed. It is hard for enemies to spot me with such a clever disguise!

My body is covered with bony plates. There are knobs and spines where the plates fit together.

This is what the plates look like in close-up.

I suck up shrimps with my long, tube-like jaws.

I am a stinging sea anemone.

I might look a bit like a flower, but I am an animal. I sit on rocks and wait for my food to pass by. I eat small fish and other creatures. I catch them in my waving tentacles.

Stinging cells in my tentacles stop my prey moving.

When I pull in my tentacles, I look like a blob of jelly.

My mouth is the hole surrounded by my tentacles.

13

I am a frilly jellyfish.

I have a jelly-like body
and I float in the sea.
My long arms are called
tentacles. I use them
to trap and eat
tiny animals.

I am harmless to
you, but beware!
Other jellyfish can give
you a nasty sting.

These tentacles can sting, and protect me from enemies.

I am a snappy scallop.

I swim by clapping the two halves of my shell together. I can shoot backwards very fast to escape from danger.

The ridges on my shell make it very strong.

The rows of black dots along the edge of my shell are my eyes.

The two halves of my shell are joined at the back. Each half is called a valve.

I am a scuttling crab.

My hard skeleton is on the
outside of my body. I have
to shed, or moult, my
skeleton in order
to grow.

I use my pincers to attack my enemies and eat my food.

My legs are made up of seven parts, with joints between them.

I have eight walking legs and two big pincers. My tail is folded under my body.

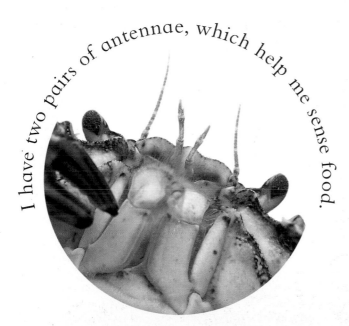

I have two pairs of antennae, which help me sense food.

I am a squirming octopus.

I have eight long arms
with rows of suckers along
them. I curl my arms
around my prey.

I am not quite as big as my picture on this page.

I use my arms for
swimming, feeding
and fighting. I eat
my food using my
beak-like jaws.

My blue circles tell you that I am very poisonous. They get brighter if I am scared or angry. My poison could kill you.

My suckers hold my prey tightly.

I stretch out my arms like this to help me zoom through the water.

19

I am a spiny starfish.

I have five flexible, bendy arms. If one of my arms is crushed or bitten off, I can grow a new one.

My tough skin and spines help to support and protect my body.

Under my arms are rows of tiny tube feet, full of water. I use these feet to glide along and to pull open the shellfish that I eat.

I can pump water into my feet, which makes them longer.

Sunstars have more legs than I do. How many legs does this one have?

I need to keep my body damp. If I am washed up on the beach, I will dry out. At low tide, I creep under rocks or hide in rock pools.

Important words

gills A collection of thin flaps that allow fish and some young amphibians to breathe under water.

moulting The shedding of the outer covering of an animal's body, which allows it to grow.

scales Thin, hard, overlapping plates that protect the skin of fish and reptiles.

skeleton A strong framework that supports an animal's body.

tentacle A long bendy structure like an arm, near an animal's mouth. It may have suckers or stings.

valve One half of the two-part shell of a shellfish, such as a scallop.

Index